BRAVO! BRAVA!

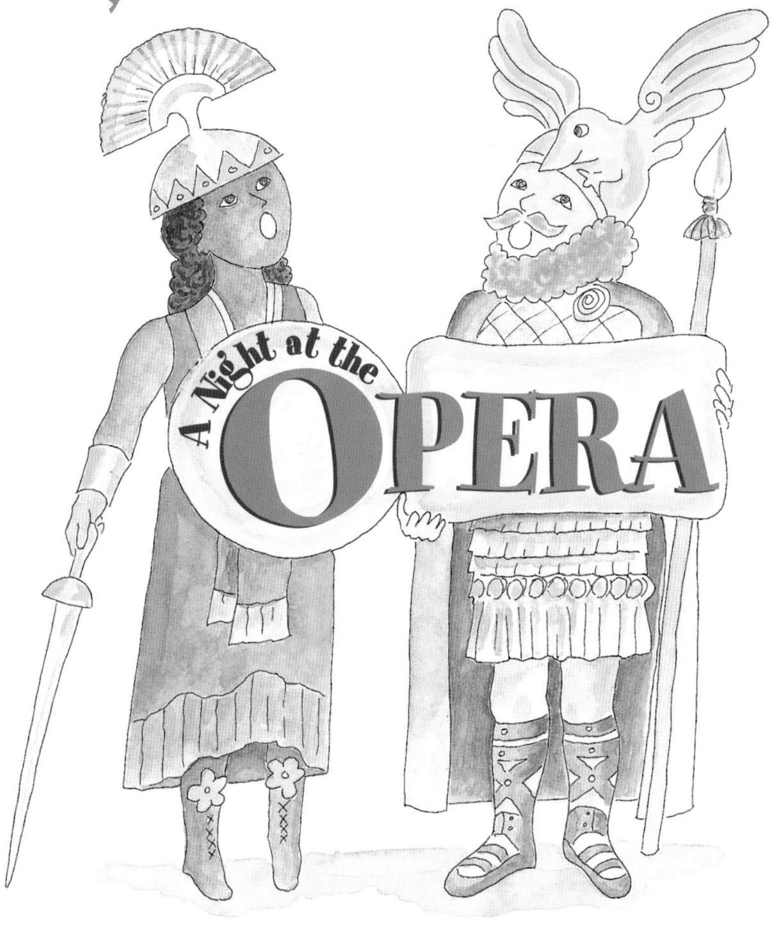

BRAVO! BRAVA!
A NIGHT
AT THE OPERA

Behind the Scenes with
Composers, Cast, and Crew

Anne Siberell

Introduction by Frederica von Stade

OXFORD

UNIVERSITY PRESS

To Peter James and George Thomas

To all in opera organizations, especially their education departments,
whose encouragement added to this project, in particular those
at the Metropolitan Opera Guild, the Lyric Opera of Chicago,
the Seattle Opera, the Los Angeles Opera, The San Francisco
Opera, and Opera America, my thanks.
And for the contributions of my sons and their spouses
and the support of my family of sisters, all music devotees, I am grateful.
I also thank Jim Roberts for his resolute assistance with research.

OXFORD
UNIVERSITY PRESS

Oxford   New York
Athens Auckland Bangkok Bogotá Buenos Aires Cape Town
Dar es Salaam Delhi Florence Hong Kong Istanbul Karachi
Kolkata Kuala Lumpur Madrid Melbourne Mexico City Mumbai Nairobi
Paris Sào Paulo Shanghai Singapore Taipei Tokyo Toronto Warsaw
with associated companies in Berlin   Ibadan

Copyright © 2001 by Anne Siberell
Published by Oxford University Press, Inc.
198 Madison Avenue, New York, NY 10016

Oxford is a registered trademark of Oxford University Press

Library of Congress Cataloging-in Publication Data
Siberell, Anne.
Bravo! brava! A night at the opera : behind the scenes with composers, cast, and crew / Anne Siberell.
p. cm.
Includes bibliographical references (p.) and index.
ISBN-13 978-0-19-513966-2
ISBN 0-19-513966-6
Opera—Juvenile literature. [1. Opera—Miscellanea. 2. Questions and answers.]
I. Title: Night at the Opera. II. Title.

ML1700.S52 2001
782.1—dc21   2001021206

9 8 7 6 5 4 3

Printed in Hong Kong on acid-free paper

Design and layout: Nora Wertz

Contents

Introduction

◆ Frederica von Stade ◆

The first opera I ever saw was in Salzburg, Austria, and it was called *Der Rosenkavalier.* I remember it very well, starting with the trip to the theater. It rains a great deal in Salzburg, and this night was no exception. My family had a Volkswagen bug, and suddenly the roof sprang a leak! We arrived at the theater disheveled and wet. Because we were late, we sat on a step in the theater, the great Salzburger Festspielhaus. From the minute the first notes of the opera sounded until the curtain closed, I don't think I moved a muscle. The first act is almost an hour and a half long, so for a 15-year-old, that was a feat!

I had never seen anything like this in my life. The sounds from the singers and the orchestra were more beautiful than anything I had ever heard. Later, I saw one of the artists in a restaurant and asked my mother if I could go in and ask for her autograph. I walked into this fancy restaurant by myself and went to her table. She was kind and beautiful, and I was thrilled. It was Elisabeth Schwarzkopf, one of the world's great sopranos, and that signature is one of my most beloved treasures.

Since then I have been moved many times by great opera singing. One moment that always comes to mind is hearing the celebrated mezzo-soprano Janet Baker in England at Glyndebourne in an opera called *The Return of Ulysses.* I could feel every word she sang and see the emotion in her face. A special light seemed to surround her and shine out from her.

When I debuted at the Metropolitan Opera in New York City, I was 23 years old and a novice to the world of opera. I had dreamed of making singing a career but never imagined singing in an opera house, especially the Metropolitan Opera! I was singing the part of a little boy, and three of us were suspended in a swing way up above the Met stage, about two stories high. We had to wait a long time until our entrance. The stagehands and the director kept telling us not to look down, which of course was the first thing we did. I was terrified, and when we were lowered to sing, my voice was shaking and it took a few moments to remember what I was supposed to do. But the thrill of singing on the stage of the Met meant so much to me. I knew that my family were there to hear me and watch me, and I felt proud and so in love with music.

My favorite part of being in opera is the feeling that you belong to a big family. Hundreds of people are often on stage at the same time, many who the public never see, working hard to make magic. We are together to make music and present a beautiful evening to the public. We singers dress up as characters that we aren't at all. We wear makeup and beautiful wigs. It's such fun. The people backstage treat us beautifully. With the reverence and demands and excitement of the opera world, it's hard to imagine that there is also a great deal of love and affection and nurturing. By the time you walk from your dressing room to the stage, you have said hello to about 25 people who are giving you their good wishes. You care about them all, and they care about you.

Where can you

see a play,

maybe
watch a ballet,

and hear
beautiful singing

accompanied
by a big
orchestra,

all at the same time?

At an opera.

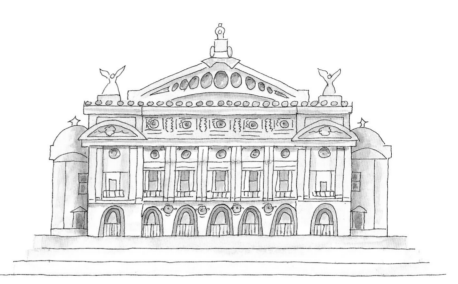

Here, you'll see scenery that's been painted and sculpted, costumes from all periods of history, and spectacular events that magically happen onstage—all held together by thrilling music. It's this combination of sight and sound that makes opera unique. Each opera you see will tell a fascinating story.

In opera, the story is told in music. The singers act out the story, but they keep on singing the whole time—whether they're falling in love, fighting, or even dying. Each production is different, so even if you know how an opera ends, there will still be surprises. Besides, every singer interprets a role differently. This is why audiences go again and again to see such favorites as *The Magic Flute, Carmen,* and *La Bohème.*

How did opera begin?

In about 1600 in Florence, Italy, some poets and musicians called the Camerata ("the group that meets in a room") wanted to start a new kind of musical entertainment. Their experiments in combining poetry and music led to opera. The oldest opera that is still performed today is *Orfeo,* written in 1607 by the Italian composer Claudio Monteverdi. The very first opera house opened in Venice in 1637.

The operas that the Italian composers wrote feature two kinds of music: *recitative* and *aria.* In recitative the characters are telling the story, either by having a conversation or describing an event. Recitative is singing that imitates the way people talk, and a harpsichord or piano usually accompanies it. In an aria, one person is expressing his or her feelings about what is happening. An aria has a more elaborate melody than recitative, and the whole orchestra joins in.

French composers, especially Jean-Baptiste Lully, started writing operas in the 1600s too, but theirs had more ballet and instrumental music in them.

English opera started out with what's called a *masque,* a combination of poetry, songs, instrumental music, dancing, and acting performed at the royal court. The greatest English composer of the 1600s was Henry Purcell. His opera *Dido and Aeneas,* which he wrote for a girls' boarding school, is still performed today.

The first opera brought to the American stage came from England all the way to South Carolina in the early 1770s. This was a ballad opera—that is, dialogue was spoken rather than sung, and the audience knew the tunes. English musicians continued to present other ballad operas in the United States, one of which was "Yankee Doodle."

Back in Italy in the 1700s, composers were writing either serious opera (called *opera seria*) or comic opera (called *opera buffa*). Other countries followed their example. George Frideric Handel, for example, a German composer living in London, wrote lots of opera seria. Germany came up with a kind of opera called *singspiel* (which means "sing speak"), with spoken dialogue rather than recitative. The most famous singspiel is *The Magic Flute,* by Wolfgang Amadeus Mozart.

Most of the operas we hear today were written in the 1800s, opera's golden age. Italy was the leader again, with the composers Gioacchino

Rossini, Gaetano Donizetti, Vincenzo Bellini, Giuseppe Verdi, and Giacomo Puccini. The stories could break your heart or tickle your funny bone, and the melodies were irresistible. Now recitatives were sometimes accompanied by the whole orchestra, just like the arias.

All through the 1800s, opera was very popular in the United States. People bought sheet music to the tunes from operas such as Mozart's *The Marriage of Figaro* and Rossini's *Cinderella* and played and sang them at home, the way we sing pop tunes today. French operas were performed in New Orleans, where many people spoke French. And in San Francisco, opera singers performed for miners who had come out West during the gold rush to try to make their fortune. The miners showed their appreciation by throwing gold nuggets onto the stage.

Toward the end of the 19th century, German composer Richard Wagner changed opera forever. In his operas, instead of recitatives and arias, the orchestra plays continuously, and singers sing throughout. There aren't any breaks in the music, as there are in earlier operas. Composers have continued to write in this way ever since.

Opera across the Pacific

In the late 1880s, Peking-opera companies in San Francisco performed for immigrants from China. Chinese opera singers wear elaborate costumes and colorful makeup, and performances have dancing and even acrobatics. Though the music in Peking opera is very different from that in Western opera, both use striking sights and sounds to inspire the audience.

	Italy	France	Austria/Germany	England
16th Century	Singer Jacopo Peri composes *Euridice*, the first opera that has survived	Baldessare da Belgioioso combines song, dance, spectacle, and drama for King Henry III		
17th Century	Venice builds the very first opera house, open to the public	Early operas include lots of ballet and fancy costumes and scenery	*Adam and Eve* by Johann Theile inaugurates the Hamburg Opera in 1678	Entertainments called *masques* feature songs, dances, instrumental music, and poetry
18th Century	Audiences cry at *opera seria* (serious) and laugh at *opera buffa* (comic)	Comic operas, with songs and spoken dialogue, are the most popular	Wolfgang Amadeus Mozart composes *The Magic Flute*, a singspiel with spoken dialogue	German composer George Frideric Handel triumphs in London with nearly 40 operas
19th Century	Gioacchino Rossini's operas usher in the age of *bel canto* (beautiful singing)	Grand operas, in five acts, feature huge casts and lavish scenery	Richard Wagner composes the *Ring*, a cycle of operas about heroes from German legends	Gilbert and Sullivan delight audiences with their funny, tuneful light operas
20th Century	Tenor Enrico Caruso thrills opera fans everywhere	Claude Debussy's *Pelléas and Mélisande* gives opera a new, delicate sound	Alban Berg contributes two powerful operas, *Wozzeck* and *Lulu*, to the repertoire	Benjamin Britten composes *Peter Grimes* and other operas with strong characters

United States

Americans hear ballad operas from England, which include familiar tunes

Soprano Jenny Lind (the "Swedish nightingale") tours the country, and crowds cheer

Gian Carlo Menotti writes *Amahl and the Night Visitors* specially for TV

Russia

Composers write operas about Russian czars or characters from Russian legends

Soviet Union bans Dmitri Shostakovich's *Lady Macbeth of Mtsensk*

Czechoslovakia

Leos Janáček's operas are based on rhythms of the Czech language

An Inspiring Story

When Italian composer Giuseppe Verdi was in his 20s, his wife and two children died, and he grew too discouraged to write music. But then a friend showed him the libretto to *Nabucco*; Verdi went to work on it, and had his first hit.

The story is about Hebrew prisoners in Old Testament Babylon. At the time Verdi was writing, the mid-19th century, Austria occupied Italy. Many Italians related to the story of captivity, and the prisoners' chorus "Va, pensiero" became their anthem. It begins "Fly, thoughts, on golden wings; go and rest on hills and dales where warm and soft are smelling the sweet auras of our native soil!"

15

Who writes the words,
and who writes the music?

The words to an opera are called a libretto. This means a "little book" of the words that are spoken and sung in the opera. The person who writes the libretto is called a librettist. The composer writes the music. Sometimes composers write the words too. The German composer Richard Wagner not only wrote his own libretto for *The Ring of the Nibelung* (a group of four operas), he even built an opera house!

When opera was first developing in Europe, people were eager for stories, and the libretto was the most important part. Sometimes different composers used the same libretto. But when great composers began to write for opera, audiences fell in love with the music. They began to idolize the singers and marvel at what they could do with their voices. An opera's arias were like a musical showpiece for the singers. Between arias, audiences talked, flirted, played cards or chess, and ate snacks.

The librettist decides what will happen in each scene and what words the singers will speak or sing. The composer takes these words and sets them to music that lets us know what the characters are feeling, what kind of people they are. To the librettist, characters are the heroine, the bad guy, and so on. To the composer, they are also voices: soprano, mezzo-soprano, tenor, baritone, or bass.

Librettists get their stories from a variety of sources. *Cinderella* and *Hansel and Gretel* are based on fairy tales. The novels *Billy Budd* by Herman Melville and *Carmen* by Prosper Mérimée have been retold as operas. Events in the lives of historical figures such as the Roman general *Julius Caesar* or the Russian czar *Boris Godunov* have been turned into opera plots, and so have myths, as in *Tristan and Isolde*, and Bible stories, as in *Amahl and the Night Visitors*. Italian composer Giuseppe Verdi and librettist Arrigo Boito worked together to make Shakespeare's play *Othello* into an opera (*Otello* in Italian). They reduced 3,500 lines of poetry to 800 for the libretto.

Composers translate action and emotion into music in a dramatic way, so that we're caught up in the story. They decide how large the orchestra will be, what instruments to use, what voices to use, and how many singers. Although Verdi and Boito drastically shortened Shakespeare's play, the basic story of Othello, his wife Desdemona, and the wicked Iago and the story's themes—good and evil, honesty and deception—come through powerfully in Verdi's music.

Opera for Special Occasions

In 1625 Francesca Caccini, a singer and composer in Florence, Italy, wrote an opera to honor a visiting prince from Poland.

Slow Composers, Fast Composers

Gioacchino Rossini wrote *The Barber of Seville* in only 13 days. Ludwig van Beethoven wrote only one opera, *Fidelio*, but he revised it over a period of 9 years before he was satisfied.

17

◆ WHAT YOU CAN EXPECT IN OPERA STORIES ◆

Suspense!

Comedy!

Madness!

Love!

Tragedy!

Horror!

War!

18

Some people say opera is boring, probably because most librettos were written in languages we don't understand. But today many opera houses provide English translations on a screen above the stage or on the back of the seat in front of you. You can also follow the plot better if you read the story of the opera, or a *synopsis*, before you go to see it. You can find synopses in books, on the Web, or in the program notes to an opera recording, which you can get at a library or record store.

Norway
The Flying Dutchman

Russia
Boris Godunov

Bohemia
The Bartered Bride

see
inset

China
Turandot

Japan
Madama
Butterfly

Cyprus
Otello

Judea
Amahl and
the Night
Visitors

Egypt
Aida

**Ceylon
(Sri Lanka)**
The Pearl Fishers

Fairy Kingdom
A Midsummer
Night's Dream

Undersea Kingdom
Sadko

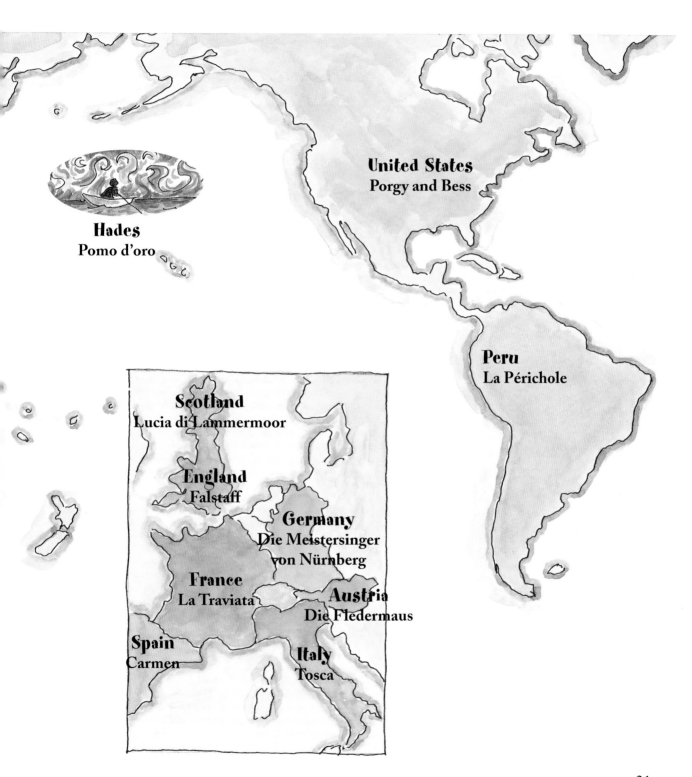

Hades
Pomo d'oro

United States
Porgy and Bess

Peru
La Périchole

Scotland
Lucia di Lammermoor

England
Falstaff

Germany
Die Meistersinger
von Nürnberg

France
La Traviata

Austria
Die Fledermaus

Spain
Carmen

Italy
Tosca

Who makes an opera happen?

GENERAL DIRECTOR

The general director of an opera house has to plan the list of operas that will be produced during a "season" years in advance. (A season is the time of the year when operas are presented, usually from the fall to the spring.) If the general director wants certain singers to appear in these operas, she needs to make sure they will be available and willing to perform. Great singers have busy schedules and are often booked for several years in advance. Opera is one of the most international of the arts—singers, conductors, directors, and designers travel all over the world to be part of an opera.

MUSIC DIRECTOR/CONDUCTOR

After the director chooses the season's operas, she meets with the principal conductor, or a guest conductor, who will set the mood of an opera through the music. The conductor, called "Maestro," or master, will interpret the score, deciding, for example, how fast or slow the music should be. He can also choose between different versions of one opera. For instance, Verdi wrote both five-act and four-act versions of *Don Carlos.*

STAGE DIRECTOR

The stage director is responsible for what happens onstage. He tells the singers how to move—when to walk from stage left to stage right, when to enter through a door, and so on—and helps them understand the characters they are playing. If the stage is full of singers, chorus members, dancers and sometimes animals, it can be tricky to keep the action moving without people bumping into each other. One opera that was performed back in the 1600s in Italy had 400 people, 2 lions, 2 elephants, several hundred horses, and an onstage stable filled with wild boar, deer, and bears.

SET DESIGNER

For each opera, the general director selects a set designer, who will design the sets and scenery and decide how the whole production looks. The designer usually knows about building and how a theater works backstage. He will work with the lighting designer.

Months before the production, the designer meets with the stage director to get his ideas for the opera. Maybe the stage director wants to make an opera like Rossini's *Cinderella* look like it's taking place in an American city. The designer might make a little model of how the stage will look so that everyone involved in the production will know what the finished set will look like. The designer and stage director also meet with the conductor to make sure the design works with the music making.

Soprano Takes a Spill

Sometimes the stage director asks singers to do difficult things. For instance, the Czech soprano Maria Jeritza, a glamorous star in the 1920s, had to roll down 20 steps for her final scene in a production of *Carmen.*

23

Who holds an opera performance together?

That's the conductor. She signals the singers and musicians when it's their turn to sing or play and makes sure the orchestra doesn't play too loud so the audience can hear the singers. A conductor must be ready for any unexpected trouble onstage. Anything can happen. A curtain may rise or fall at the wrong time, a trapdoor may refuse to open, a singer may start on the wrong note, a dancer may fall down. The conductor keeps things

Perils...

In the 17th century, French composer Jean-Baptiste Lully struck himself in the foot with the cane he was using to beat time on the floor. He died from this wound three months later.

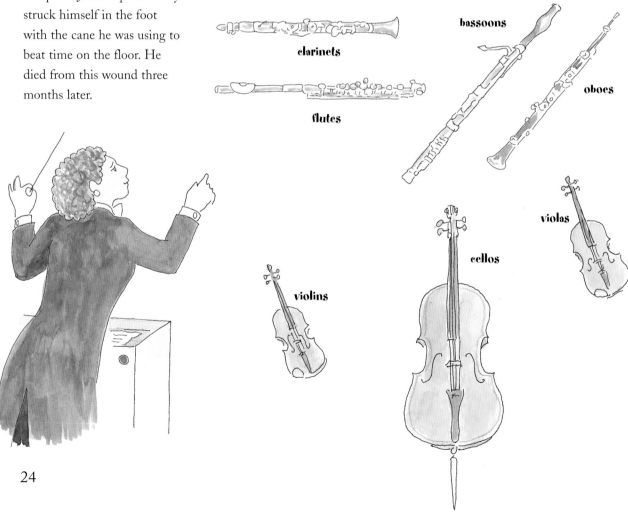

clarinets

flutes

bassoons

oboes

violas

cellos

violins

24

moving, so the audience may not even know anything is wrong.

The conductor leads the orchestra, musicians who play together as a team. Conductors can usually play at least one instrument, but they know how all the instruments work. Occasionally, one musician may play a solo passage. The players wear black so that they will blend into the darkness below the stage. The area where they sit is called a pit. Sometimes it is covered. The orchestra pit can be so crowded that the musicians bump each other with their instruments, or that brass players accidentally spit on woodwind players!

...and Pitfalls

At an outdoor production of *Carmen* with 38 horses on stage, a horse startled by the conductor's sudden upbeat flew into the orchestra pit with its rider and onto the kettledrums.

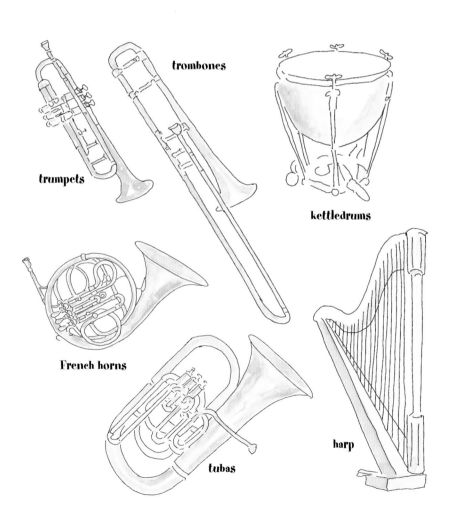

trombones

trumpets

kettledrums

French horns

tubas

harp

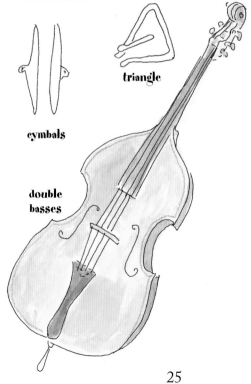

cymbals

triangle

double basses

25

Dishes for Divas

Chefs in elegant restaurants have named dishes after opera stars. Australian soprano Nellie Melba inspired peach Melba (a dessert made with peaches, ice cream, and raspberry sauce) and melba toast (very thin toast). Chicken tetrazzini (a spaghetti dish) was created for Italian soprano Luisa Tetrazzini.

Who is on the stage?

On the stage, the most important singers are called the principals, or stars. A female star is also called by the Italian terms "prima donna" or "diva"; a man is called "divo." Singers are cast by their vocal range, which determines the kind of role they'll play. Usually a soprano with a sweet, high voice will be the heroine, maybe someone's daughter, and a baritone with a deep, powerful voice will be her father. If the two of them are singing together it is called a duet. If one is singing alone, that is a solo aria. Three voices are a trio, and four a quartet.

Up to the 1820s the public loved performers for their "bel canto," which means "beautiful singing." They seemed to be able to do anything with their voices—they could sing high notes and low notes and all the notes in between at a very fast pace (a way of singing called "coloratura"). But over time, opera fans wanted more than just technique—they wanted songs sung with feeling.

A soprano from Sweden named Jenny Lind made a big splash in the United States when she toured the country from 1850 to 1852. She was known as the "Swedish nightingale." When her ship arrived in New York harbor, a crowd of 30,000 people greeted her. At her concerts, she sang arias from operas but also songs the audience knew, like "Home, Sweet Home." At one outdoor concert in New York, 6,000 people came to hear her, and those who couldn't get in bobbed around in boats on a lake that surrounded the theater, listening.

Popular opera singers today may travel all over the world in a single year, singing one role maybe in Milan, Italy, another in

Vienna, Austria, another in Paris, France, and still another in New York, Chicago, Santa Fe, or St. Louis. Experienced singers are able to sing in Italian, French, German, English, and sometimes even Russian or Czech. In earlier times a conductor might rehearse with the singers for months before the opera season. Now, with tight travel schedules, the conductor rehearses soloists as they arrive at the opera house. Before the final dress rehearsal the conductor meets with all the principal singers and full orchestra. The soloists sit on stage above the orchestra pit dressed in comfortable clothes and sing the whole opera together.

Who is under the stage?

Onstage anyone can forget the words or notes, especially if they know from 20 to 100 opera roles and are suffering from jet lag or are in a new opera house. The prompter is there in case this happens. She climbs up a little ladder and squeezes into a little box (the size of a phone booth) partly under the stage at the very front, facing the singers. The audience can just see the top of this box. The prompter has the music in front of her and watches a TV monitor that shows the conductor. Once the opera has started, she can mouth the next words a singer has to sing.

◆ VOCAL RANGES ◆

Papageno
The Magic Flute

Otello
Otello

Mephistopheles
Faust

Bass
Lowest range for men;
kings, priests, villains

Baritone
Middle range for men;
villains, companions,
sometimes heroes

Tenor
High range for men;
usually the hero

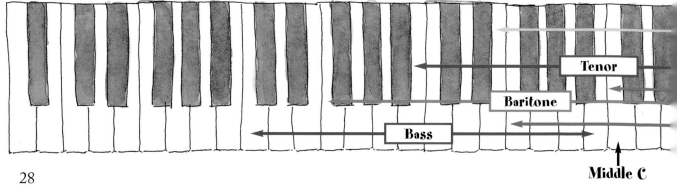

Tenor

Baritone

Bass

Middle C

Oberon
A Midsummer Night's Dream

Witch
Hansel and Gretel

Baba the Turk
The Rake's Progress

Olympia
Tales of Hoffmann

Countertenor
Highest range for men;
men's roles in early operas
(from the 1600s
and 1700s)

Contralto or Alto
Lowest range for women;
old women, witches,
comic characters

Mezzo-Soprano
Middle range for women;
often mothers, older
women, young men or
boys. When a woman plays
a male character, it is called
a *trouser role.*

Soprano
High range for women;
usually the heroine

29

BALLET

Some operas include a ballet (these performers just dance; they don't sing). In the mid-1800s, the French were used to seeing a ballet as part of their musical entertainment, so when Wagner presented his opera *Tannhäuser* in Paris, he wrote a ballet into the first act. Then he was told to put the ballet in the second act, because the "important" people always came late to the theater. He refused, and when high society sat through the second act and saw no ballet, they hissed and booed, and the performance ended in a riot.

Another famous ballet takes place in Verdi's *Aida*, in a spectacular scene where the stage is filled with people, chariots, and even animals.

THE CHORUS

Though the singers in the chorus usually support the principal singers, they are also highly trained and accomplished. Chorus members have to memorize music sung in several foreign languages. In addition to singing, they dance, march, take part in the action onstage, and react to whatever happens in the opera.

CHILDREN

Some operas feature a chorus of children—examples are Georges Bizet's *Carmen*, Engelbert Humperdinck's *Hansel and Gretel*, and Giacomo Puccini's *La Bohème*. These children are chosen from choruses in schools or the community, or they might come from families of singers. In Gian Carlo Menotti's *Amahl and the Night Visitors*, one of the principal roles is for a young boy.

SUPERNUMERARIES

Supernumeraries, or supers, don't sing, dance, or have speaking parts. They play walk-on roles: guards, priests, students, townspeople, prisoners, street vendors, travelers, soldiers, children, peasants, ladies-in-waiting, nobles, servants, party guests, and whatever else an opera calls for. They are often jokingly called "spear carriers." Though supers spend many hours in costume fittings and makeup sessions and rehearsals, they are paid mostly in the satisfaction of taking part in an opera. Plus they might get to stand next to a superstar.

Who is backstage, behind the curtain?

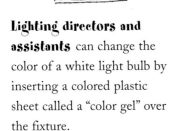

Lighting directors and assistants can change the color of a white light bulb by inserting a colored plastic sheet called a "color gel" over the fixture.

Upholsterers make furniture and draperies that tell when the story is taking place. For *Aida*, these workers are using fabrics with bright patterns popular in ancient Egypt.

Stagehands use pin rails to secure the ropes that they pull and release to raise and lower curtains and pieces of scenery.

Scenic artists build and paint scenery to show where the story is taking place. These artists are making a sphinx, an ancient Egyptian image.

Prop people collect or create all the things the actors will need to make the performance look real, except for costumes and painted scenery.

33

After the general director approves the design plans, the sketches and models of the design are sent to the technical department. These are the people backstage, behind the curtain. The costume designer, lighting designer, and makeup and wig artists make their own sketches and plans. The carpenters, sculptors, and painters build sets that the designer has designed.

Layers of curtains cover these illusions. In some opera houses, the curtain hiding the stage is an elegant one. The gold curtain at the San Francisco Opera house is made of more than a mile of silk. Behind the gold curtain are other curtains. They each have a special purpose.

Different Stages

A trapdoor is a hidden opening, usually in the floor, used to bring actors, props, and scenery on and off stage. Sets can be easily slid on and off a slip stage, which has sideways tracks for rolling props and scenery into place. A raked stage slants upward as it goes back, so that the audience can see the performers. A revolving stage is useful for making scene changes. The settings are built on a turntable that spins slowly into place.

trapdoor

slip stage

raked stage

revolving stage

◆ CURTAINS ◆

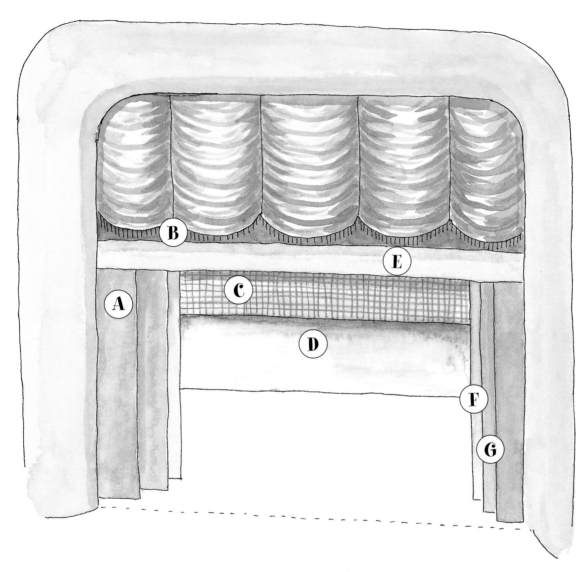

A. **Tormentors** These long curtains conceal the wings, lights, and places called "flies," where scenery and equipment are hung.

B. **Fire Curtain** This heat-activated curtain provides fire protection and soundproofing.

C. **Scrim** The scrim is see-through when lit from behind, and you can't see through it when it's lit from the front. Lights and film projected on it can create clouds, wind, mist, sun, or even falling buildings.

D. **Cyclorama** This backdrop screen is for deep backgrounds like the sky. A cyclorama can be almost the size of a football field. Light projected on it from the rear or wings creates special effects.

E. **Teaser** This curtain inside the arch, or proscenium, covers the top of the stage.

F. **Legs** These side curtains are usually used in ballet.

G. **Traveler** This curtain, usually black or gold, is held open for curtain calls.

STAGE MANAGER

The stage manager oversees everything that happens backstage. She's like a traffic cop. She wears a headset and stands at a console with a musical score (all the notes and words in the opera). She can see the conductor and the entire stage on different TV monitors, and she's able to communicate with all the performers and stagehands.

The stage manager can read music and understands how computers, machinery, and lighting work. She's present at all stage rehearsals, so she knows what needs to happen: when singers are supposed to enter and exit, when the sets change (maybe one scene takes place in a drawing room and the next in a fancy palace), when the lights change, and the exact note on which the curtains open and close. In an action-packed opera like Sergey Prokofiev's *War and Peace*, she pushes certain buttons to make cannons go off, smoke billow, walls crumble, and ballroom lights shine. She also cues the electricians perched high above the stage, who operate the spotlights.

The stage manager keeps in touch with artists in their dressing rooms. By talking into their "squawk boxes," she tells them how much time is left before they have to go on—30 minutes, 20 minutes, 10 minutes, then a red light comes on to signal the 5-minute warning. Finally, "Places!" she says, and the performers take their places onstage.

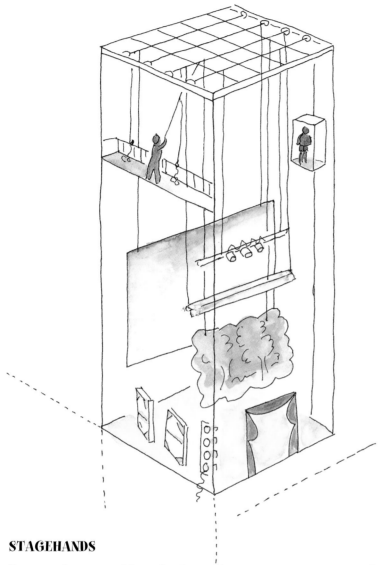

Flagrant Fowl

The Austrian tenor Leo Slezak finished singing his "Farewell" in *Lohengrin* and went over to the swan-drawn boat that was to carry him offstage. When the stagehands moved the boat before he could get on it, Slezak walked toward the audience and politely asked, "Tell me, please, what time is the next swan?"

STAGEHANDS

It can take several hundred people to put on an opera. Among those people are the stagehands, men and women who work in hidden areas of the stage changing scenery and props between scenes and creating special effects.

Special effects have happened onstage for hundreds of years. For an opera performed in Venice in 1645, workers operated machines that hoisted singers and musicians up to the clouds. The shipwrecks, fireworks, lightning, explosions,

37

battles, daring stunts, fires, and floods that have always been a part of opera are, with the latest technology, more convincing than ever.

Weather effects can be achieved through screen projections and sound recordings. Fog, mist, and smoke onstage come from hoses that are attached to a container of dry ice. If it's fog, portable fans disperse the fog into the air. It stays on the stage with the help of a grill in the floor of the stage that lets in air from the basement and holds back the fog. Snow is made out of white shredded paper or plastic (confetti) placed in a long paper bag that stretches across the top of the stage. Stagehands spill the confetti into a tray with holes in it, then rock the tray back and forth above the stage—presto, it's snowing! To make rain, a V-shaped trough as wide as the stage is placed above the stage. A stagehand feeds the water from hoses, and a valve in the trough releases water on cue. A drain carries the water from the stage. A stagehand makes thunder by turning a revolving handle on a machine that bellows out a boom of thunder, or by playing a recording.

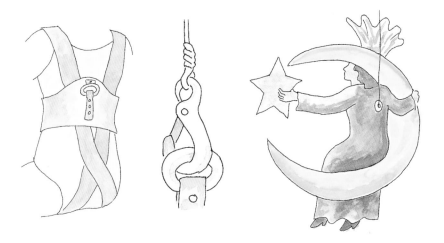

LIGHTING DESIGNER AND TECHNICIANS

Sunrise, sunset, moonlight, spooky forest spirits—in opera, all these depend on lighting. A tragic opera might need dark shadows for some scenes. A comic opera might use bright light to help create a happy mood. A lighting designer for *La Bohème* has to create moonlight, dawn, and shafts of sunlight. Three quarters of *Don Giovanni* takes place in the dark, but the lighting designer needs to create this effect while still allowing the audience to see what's happening.

As many as 600 lights might be used for a performance, and there are all kinds, ranging from a simple bulb to airport runway lights. And lighting equipment in an opera is not just restricted to lights. Designers use color gels, film projectors, superimposed images, strobe lighting, and other means to achieve the effects they want.

Once the lighting designer has chosen the lighting for an opera, the required combinations of spotlights and dimmers are entered into a computer. The number of combinations can be enormous, and some are complicated. During a performance, the stage manager signals the light changes to the light booth, where a technician mans the computer. A single console may control 400 spotlights.

39

THE COSTUME DESIGNER AND CREW

The costumes we see as soon as the curtain rises tell us the time in history of the story we're about to see and hear. They can also help set the mood of the opera. The costume designer studies clothing of the period and country where each opera takes place, then designs costumes for the production.

When she completes the designs, she sends them to the costume shop to be made. The costumes are sturdily made so they will last through years of wearing. In fact, designers talk about "building" costumes. Since opera singers come in all shapes and sizes, the costumes have seams that are wide enough to alter to fit each singer in the role. In early opera, stars owned their costumes. Some still do.

Cotton, silk, and linen are often used, because these fabrics are more comfort-

able under hot lights than synthetic fabrics, especially if a singer is wearing padding to look fat! Under their costumes, performers wear flesh-colored cotton T-shirts that absorb the sweat. Washing machines and dryers are kept busy in opera houses.

Since 150 to 500 costumes might be used for a single opera, people in the costume shop prepare many bolts of fabric for sewing. Some opera houses have spraying rooms and dyeing rooms, with vats holding various colors. That's where mud and blood are spattered onto costumes for operas that feature battle scenes or other gory events. In the second act of *Falstaff,* the title character hides in a basket of laundry, only to be thrown out with the wash into the River Thames. He gets soaked and muddy, and sometimes a costume designer uses rocks in Falstaff's pockets to weigh down his coat and make him look rumpled.

Siegfried

Ring of the Nibelung

Rigoletto

Rigoletto

Violetta

La Traviata

Canio

Pagliacci

Cio-Cio-San

Madama Butterfly

Angelina

Cinderella

43

MAKEUP ARTISTS AND WIG MASTERS

In opera, singers are cast for their voices, not how they look. So how can a young singer look old? Makeup can do wonders.

In Verdi's *Aida*, everyone has to have an Egyptian skin tone. And since this opera has a large cast of dancers, slaves, priests, priestesses, prisoners, guards, and other Egyptians, up to 30 makeup artists might be "doing a face" at one time.

On the opera stage, even if the performer's hair looks real, it probably isn't. Almost everyone wears a wig. Each wig is colored and dyed to suit the character in the opera.

To make a wig, the wig artist begins by taking a measurement of the performer's head. He makes a cap of vegetable netting—a frame for the

Giants
Ring of the Nibelung

Samson
Samson and Delilah

Wig Work

It can take 40 hours to make a wig, and there can be more than 100 wigs in one opera.

hairpiece called a "lace." He weaves strands of hair one at a time with an instrument like a tiny crochet hook and knots each piece. The weaving is called "ventilating," and the silk ribbon he uses is called "galloon." The wigmaster uses human hair or yak hair. Wigs can be black, brown, red, or white (powdered wigs were worn in the 18th century, for example). Artists wash the hair after each performance, then comb, brush, fluff, and spray it again.

Ping, Pang, and Pong
Turandot

Octavian
Der Rosenkavalier

Mélisande
Pelléas and Mélisande

How do they all come together?

After many rehearsals, the lead singers, chorus, conductor, orchestra, scenery, lighting, costumes, makeup, wigs, ballet, stage director, stage manager, prompter, and technical crew all come together. The stars rest or sing warm-ups in their dressing rooms. The stage manager calls "10 minutes," then "5 minutes" before raising the curtain. Dressers help singers put on costumes and make the stars comfortable while they're waiting, then lead them through backstage corridors to the stage.

When you finally arrive at the opera house for the big night, an usher shows you to your seat. The orchestra tunes up, the house lights dim, and the conductor comes out and takes a bow. Sometimes the orchestra plays an overture before the curtain rises; this sets the mood of the opera.

In the early days of opera, fans would throw oranges at a star they didn't like.

Opera audiences tend to express their feelings openly (this is part of the fun). After a singer has sung a beautiful or difficult aria especially well, they might burst into applause and yell "Brava!" (if it's a woman) or "Bravo!" (if it's a man). They might even boo or hiss a singer or the conductor. Mostly, though, everyone in the opera and the audience is happy with

the miracle of a great performance, made possible by hundreds of people working together. Sometimes curtain calls go on for 20 minutes or more after the opera has ended. Opera fans will be back for another performance, because they know that every time at an opera is a new and exciting experience. It will be for you, too.

Glossary

aria A musical piece for one singer

bel canto "Beautiful singing"

chorus A group of singers

coloratura A style of singing that's usually fast, with lots of notes, including ornamentation (notes the singer adds)

diva A female singing star

divo A male singing star

duet A musical piece for two voices

librettist The person who writes the text of an opera

libretto The words to an opera

opera buffa Comic opera

opera seria Serious opera

overture Music played by the orchestra before an opera begins

program Sheet of paper or booklet that gives information about the opera

prompter The person in a booth at the foot of the stage who gives singers cues

proscenium "Before stage"; the area framing the stage

quartet A musical piece for four voices

raked stage A slanted floor, higher in back than in front

recitative Dialogue that is sung in between arias, usually accompanied by a harpsichord or piano rather than orchestra

rehearsal Practice before a performance

repertory The collection of roles a singer has learned

score A printed sheet with the words and music of an opera

scrim Sheer cloth used as a backdrop or transparent curtain

synopsis The story of an opera

tempo The speed of a musical piece

trio Musical piece for three voices

Favorite Opera Plots

Georges Bizet (1838–75)
French

Carmen (1875)

19th-century Seville, Spain. Micaëla comes to the town square to find her soldier sweetheart, Don José. When the girls working at a cigarette factory come outside for a break, the soldiers especially admire the gypsy Carmen, who sings a song about love. Later, she gets into a fight with another girl and is arrested. Don José is her guard, and he falls in love with her and lets her escape.

Two months later, Carmen is with her gypsy friends at a camp when Don José arrives, now a deserter from the army. Micaëla arrives at the camp and begs Don José to return to his ill mother, which he does. Escamillo, a bullfighter, is also in love with Carmen, and now she's attracted to him, too. At a square outside the bull ring, Don José returns to plead with Carmen to stay with him, but she says it's all over between them. Don José then stabs her, and cries that he has killed her.

Gaetano Donizetti (1797–1848)
Italian

L'elisir d'amore
(The Elixir of Love, 1832)

19th-century Italy. Farm worker Nemorino is in love with the wealthy owner of the farm, Adina. Soldiers arrive in town, and one of them, the silly Sergeant Belcore, decides he wants to marry Adina. Dr. Dulcamara comes to town selling miracle medicines. Nemorino asks him for a love potion, and the doctor sells him a bottle that really only holds ordinary wine. Nemorino drinks it, becomes drunk, and ignores Adina. Belcore asks Adina to marry him, and to get even with Nemorino, Adina says yes.

Meanwhile, Nemorino's rich uncle has died and left him all his money. The village girls hear about this and start flirting with Nemorino. But Nemorino hasn't heard the news; he's drunk with the wine again and thinks the magic love potion is working. Dr. Dulcamara tells Adina the potion is making all the girls love Nemorino, and tries to sell her one, too. But Adina says she'll rely on her own charms, and tells Nemorino she loves him. Belcore thinks all the girls love him, so he doesn't mind that he can't marry Adina after all. Everyone rushes to get some of that famous love potion from Dr. Dulcamara.

Lucia di Lammermoor (1835)

Scotland, in the 17th century. Though they are from families who are bitter enemies, Lucia of Lammermoor and Edgardo of Ravenswood are in love. They meet in a forest, and Edgardo says he plans to leave for France, but then he wants to ask her brother Enrico for permission to marry her. While he's gone, Enrico arranges for Lucia to marry Arturo. Enrico shows Lucia a letter he says is from Edgardo (but it really isn't) saying that Edgardo gives Lucia up. Lucia just wants to die then, but she agrees to marry Arturo.

At the wedding, Edgardo unexpectedly returns and declares that he loves Lucia, but Lucia has to admit that she signed the marriage contract. Later, the chaplain rushes in to say that Lucia has stabbed Arturo. Lucia enters, and it's clear to all the guests that she's gone mad. Enrico realizes that he's responsible. Lucia dies, and Edgardo, in despair, kills himself.

George Gershwin (1898–1937)
American

Porgy and Bess (1935)

1920s, Catfish Row, a black neighborhood in the South. Bess is Crown's girlfriend. Crown kills his neighbor Robbins in a card game fight and leaves town. Bess has no place to go, so Porgy, a cripple, lets her stay at his house. Porgy and Bess fall in love. Sportin' Life, a drug dealer,

tries to persuade Bess to come with him to New York, but Porgy sends him away.

All the neighbors go on a picnic to an island, where Crown is hiding; there, he forces Bess to stay with him. After two days, Bess is brought back to Porgy's house, sick. Crown returns and tries to get to Bess, but Porgy strangles him and is led away. Sportin' Life finally talks Bess into going with him to New York. Porgy is released a week later and returns to find that Bess is gone. He sets off on his cart to find her.

Charles Gounod (1818–93)
French

Faust (1859)

16th-century Germany. In his old age, the scholar Faust wants to be young again. Mephistopheles (the devil) appears and offers to make Faust young in return for his soul. Faust agrees, and he and Mephistopheles set off for a tavern, where Mephistopheles shows off his supernatural powers.

Faust sees and falls in love with the beautiful Marguerite, who, with the encouragement of Mephistopheles, returns his love. But after some time has passed, we see Marguerite at her spinning wheel, sad because Faust has left her. She's had a child and is scorned by her town. Her brother Valentin attacks Faust, and Faust, with the help of Mephistopheles, kills him. Marguerite is put in prison for killing her child, and Mephistopheles leads Faust to see her. She's happy to see him, and Faust and Mephistopheles ask her to come with them. But then Marguerite realizes that Mephistopheles is the devil and refuses. Angels carry her to heaven and safety, while Faust must remain with Mephistopheles.

Roméo et Juliette
(Romeo and Juliet, 1867)

15th-century Italy. The Montagues and Capulets are families that are bitter enemies. At a dance given by the Capulets, Juliet Capulet arrives with her cousin Tybalt. Romeo Montague and his friend Mercutio enter the ballroom secretly. Romeo sees Juliet, and immediately they fall in love. That night, as Juliet leans down from her balcony, they declare their love for each other, in spite of their families' bitterness.

Later, Romeo and Juliet ask Friar Laurence to marry them, which he does. Mercutio and Tybalt get into a fight outside the Capulet house, and Tybalt kills Mercutio. Romeo, in revenge, then kills Tybalt. Romeo is banished from the town, and a marriage is arranged between Juliet and Count Paris.

Friar Laurence gives Juliet a liquid potion and tells her that when she takes it, she will look like she's dead; then when he wakes her up, she can join Romeo. Juliet takes the potion, but Romeo finds her before Friar Laurence does. Thinking she has died, he takes poison. Juliet wakes up, sees Romeo is dying, and stabs herself as they embrace for the last time.

Engelbert Humperdinck (1854–1921)
German

Hänsel und Gretel
(Hansel and Gretel, 1893)

Germany, in the age of fairy tales. Hansel and Gretel are making brooms in their house, but grow bored and start dancing. Their mother comes home and gets angry when she sees they're not working. So she sends them to the forest to hunt for berries. Hansel and Gretel get lost in the forest and fall asleep. In the morning, they find a house made of candy, surrounded by gingerbread children. As they're taking bites out of the delicious house, the wicked witch who lives there captures them and locks Hansel up; she plans to fatten him up and then cook him. But the children outwit the witch and push her into the oven. The gingerbread children come to life, and Hansel and Gretel's parents arrive and give thanks that their children are safe.

Ruggero Leoncavallo (1857–1919)
Italian

Pagliacci (1892)

19th-century Italy. In a village square, strolling players prepare to perform a play. The hunchback Tonio loves Nedda, the wife of their leader, Canio. But Nedda plans to leave that night with Silvio, a farmer who lives in the village. Tonio brings Canio to watch a meeting take place between Nedda and Silvio. Canio rushes forward with a dagger, but Beppa, another player, reminds him that they have a show to put on.

As the players act out a story similar to the one that's going on in real life, Canio, as the character Pagliaccio, loses control and stabs Nedda and Silvio. The audience grabs Canio, and Tonio announces that their comedy has ended.

Gian Carlo Menotti (b. 1911)
American

Amahl and the Night Visitors (1951)

1st-century Judaea. Amahl is a poor, crippled shepherd boy who lives with his mother in a hut. As they're falling asleep one night, there's a knock at the door. Amahl tells his mother there are three kings outside, with treasure, but she doesn't believe him. Then she goes to the door, and there are indeed three kings with their page, who ask if they can spend the night in the hut. They explain to the mother that they are taking gifts to a newborn child, and a bright star is showing them the way. Amahl brings in some neighbors, who offer the kings food and then leave.

When the kings are asleep, the mother tries to take some of the gold. The page sees her and shouts, and everyone wakes up. One of the kings says she can keep the gold, for the child they're visiting won't need it—he'll bring a new life to the world. But the mother tells him to take the gold to this child. Amahl says the child may need his crutch someday; as he offers it to the kings, he discovers that he can walk. Overjoyed, Amahl decides to go with the kings so he can give the crutch to the child himself.

Wolfgang Amadeus Mozart (1756–91)
Austrian

Così fan tutte
(Women Are Like That, 1790)

18th-century Italy. Ferrando is engaged to Dorabella, and Guglielmo is engaged to Fiordiligi; the two girls are sisters. The bachelor Don Alfonso says that women can't be trusted, and makes a bet with Ferrando and Guglielmo that their fiancées can't be faithful. He comes up with a plan, and asks the sisters' maid, Despina, to help.

Ferrando and Guglielmo pretend to go off to war, but then they return, disguised as Albanians. They say they're in love with the sisters—this time, Ferrando says he loves Fiordiligi, and Guglielmo says he loves Dorabella. The girls resist them at first, but when the men threaten to kill themselves, they agree to marry the Albanians. Despina, disguised as a judge, makes them sign a marriage contract. Then Ferrando and Guglielmo return as themselves, and the girls are in a panic. But Don Alfonso shows them how the Albanians were really their sweethearts, and the lovers are reunited.

Don Giovanni (1787)

18th-century Seville, Spain. Don Giovanni, who loves women and then leaves them, is forcing his attentions on Donna Anna. Her father, the Commendatore, comes to her rescue, but Don Giovanni kills him in a duel. Donna Anna and her fiancé, Don Octavio, vow to seek revenge. A former lover of Don Giovanni's, Donna Elvira, also vows to get even.

In the countryside near Don Giovanni's castle, the don and his servant, Leoporello, come upon Zerlina and Masetto, who have become engaged. Don Giovanni invites them to his castle, where he flirts with Zerlina. Now five people are angry at him. As Don Giovanni is preparing to enjoy dinner at his castle, Donna Elvira, who still loves him, urges him to repent. A visitor appears at the door. It's the statue of the Commendatore, which has come to life. The statue takes Don Giovanni's hand and demands that he repent, but the don is unafraid and refuses. As smoke and flames rise, Don Giovanni is dragged down to hell. The others sing that he has found his true reward.

Die Zauberflöte
(The Magic Flute, 1791)

Mythical Egypt. In a forest where the Queen of the Night rules, the queen's three ladies-in-waiting give Prince Tamino a portrait of the queen's daughter, the princess Pamina. Tamino falls in love with the picture, and the queen tells him he can marry Pamina, but first he must rescue her from the evil Sarastro. The three ladies give him a magic flute for protection, and they give his funny pal Papageno, a bird catcher, a magic glockenspiel.

Tamino discovers that Sarastro isn't really evil. He's been keeping Pamina for her own protection because her mother is the evil one. Sarastro tells Tamino that in order to win Pamina, he must prove that he's brave and wise. First, he's not allowed to speak, even to Pamina when he meets her. He passes that test, and Sarastro allows Pamina to join him for his final test. The lovers set out on a walk that passes through fire and water, as Tamino plays his magic flute to keep them safe. Papageno, with the help of his magic glockenspiel, finds what he has long been looking for—a wife, who's called Papagena. Sarastro declares that the rule of the Queen of the Night is over.

Le nozze di Figaro
(The Marriage of Figaro, 1786)

18th-century Seville, Spain. Figaro and Susanna, servants of Count and Countess Almaviva, are about to get married. The count, though, has his eye on Susanna, and the housekeeper Marcellina wants to marry Figaro. The young page Cherubino flirts with both Susanna and the countess. Figaro, Susanna, the countess, and Cherubino all conspire to play tricks on the count, which don't really work out. Figaro and Marcellina discover that she's really his long-lost mother.

Susanna and Figaro marry. That same night in the garden, Susanna and the countess disguise themselves as each other, to fool the count into thinking that Susanna wants to meet him there. Figaro is at first confused and angry when he sees a servant who he thinks is Susanna proclaiming her love for the count. But everything works out, Susanna and Figaro are united for good, and the count begs forgiveness from the countess.

Jacques Offenbach (1819–80)
French

Les Contes d'Hoffmann
(Tales of Hoffmann, 1881)

19th-century Germany. In a tavern, Hoffmann's friends are talking about his romance with Stella, an opera singer. Lindorf, the tavern keeper, is in love with Stella, too. When Hoffmann enters, they ask him to tell the story of his three past loves.

His first love, Olympia, supposedly the daughter of a scientist, was really a mechanical doll, invented by the scientist and Dr. Coppelius. The second love was Giuletta, a courtesan, who made Hoffmann fall in love with her and then tricked him, with the help of the magician Dapertutto. The third love, Antonia, was a young singer who was ill. Hoffmann urged her to go away with him, but Dr. Miracle told her he could cure her illness; he asked her to sing, and the effort caused her to die.

Hoffmann's friend Nicklausse realizes that Stella is all three women in one. But Hoffmann has drunk too much and falls asleep as Stella leaves the tavern with Lindorf.

In many performances, Olympia, Giuletta, and Antonia are sung by the same soprano, and Lindorf, Coppelius, Dapertutto, and Dr. Miracle are sung by the same baritone.

Giacomo Puccini (1858–1924)
Italian

La Bohème
(The Bohemians, 1896)

Paris, 1830. The poet Rodolfo and painter Marcello share a garret (a room just under the roof) with friends. It's cold, and they have no money to pay the rent. Rodolfo is working alone in the room when a young woman knocks at the door, saying her candle blew out on the stairs. Rodolfo invites her in, she tells him her name is Mimì and she's a seamstress, and they fall in love. They join Marcello at a café, where he meets his girlfriend, Musetta.

In time, Rodolfo becomes jealous and worries that a life of poverty will be bad for Mimì, who has tuberculosis. They agree to part. Later, all the friends are gathered in the garret. Musetta brings in Mimì, who is very sick. She and Rodolfo reunite in love before she dies.

La fanciulla del West
(The Girl of the Golden West, 1910)

19th-century California, during the gold rush. Minnie runs the Polka Saloon, near a gold-mining camp. The town's sheriff, Jack Rance, is in love with her. A stranger calling himself Dick Johnson comes to the saloon, and he and Minnie are attracted to each other. Johnson visits Minnie's cabin and declares his love. Rance and some others arrive, and Rance tells Minnie that Johnson is really the bandit Ramerrez, whom they're looking for. Minnie offers to play a game of poker; if Rance wins, he can have both

Minnie and Ramerrez, but if Minnie wins, she can keep her lover. Minnie wins the game by cheating.

Later, some miners capture Ramerrez, and he's about to be hanged, but Minnie rides to his rescue. She reminds the miners how she always looked after them in the saloon, even read to them. So they let Johnson go, and he and Minnie ride away.

Madama Butterfly (1904)

Early 20th-century Japan. Pinkerton, a lieutenant in the U.S. Navy, marries Cio-Cio-San, known as Madama Butterfly. One of the guests at the wedding is the American consul, Sharpless. Pinkerton tells Sharpless that he considers the marriage only temporary. When he's called away on duty, Pinkerton tells Butterfly that he will return in the spring.

Three years later, Butterfly is still waiting for him to return to her; in the meantime, their son has been born. Her loyal maid Suzuki believes Pinkerton won't come back, and Sharpless advises Butterfly to marry again. A ship arrives in the harbor, and Butterfly recognizes it as Pinkerton's and is overjoyed. But Pinkerton has brought his American wife, Kate, and he does not want to see Butterfly. Kate tells Suzuki that she and Pinkerton want to take the boy back to America. Butterfly agrees to let him go, but only if Pinkerton will come to see her. She embraces her son for the last time, then kills herself as the distressed Pinkerton arrives.

Tosca (1900)

19th-century Rome, Italy. Angelotti, an escaped political prisoner, hides in a church chapel. Soon after, his friend Cavaradossi comes to the church to paint a portrait. When Cavaradossi's lover, Tosca, arrives to see him, they plan to meet later at his villa. Cavaradossi gives Angelotti the key to his villa, saying he can hide in the garden well there.

Baron Scarpia, chief of police, is suspicious of Cavaradossi and puts him in prison. Tosca tells Scarpia where Angelotti is hiding in order to free Cavaradossi. Scarpia wants Tosca for himself, so he tells her he will stage a fake execution of Cavaradossi if she will be his lover. Tosca agrees, but after Scarpia writes a letter saying that both Tosca and Cavaradossi are free to go, she stabs him. She then rushes to the castle where her lover is being held, shows him the letter, and tells him about the fake execution plan. But when the firing squad arrives to shoot Cavaradossi, she discovers the bullets are real; Scarpia had been lying. In despair, she leaps off the castle roof.

Turandot (1926)

Peking, China, in the time of legends. Any prince wishing to marry the princess Turandot must answer three riddles correctly; if he tries and fails, he loses his head. Standing in a crowd outside the castle are an unknown prince (he's really Calaf, a prince in exile), his father, Timur, and Liu, a slave girl who loves Calaf. Calaf sees the beautiful Turandot on a balcony and falls in love. In spite of the protests of his father and Liu, Calaf decides to try to win Turandot.

Turandot, who hates men, asks him the three riddles. (The first one is

"What is born every night and dies in the morning in the human heart?" The answer is "Hope.") Calaf answers all three correctly. Then he tells Turandot that if she can discover his name before dawn, he'll give up his life for her. Officials torture Liu to make her reveal the name, but Liu stabs herself to save Calaf. Turandot is moved by her courage. Calaf kisses Turandot, then tells her his name and says he's ready to die. But Turandot, who has finally learned to feel emotion, spares him, announcing to the crowd that his name is Love.

Gioacchino Rossini (1792–1868)
Italian

La cenerentola
(Cinderella, 1817)

Late 18th-century Italy. Angelina works as a maid for her two snobbish stepsisters and her stepfather, Don Magnifico, who treat her badly. Prince Ramiro, who is looking for a wife, arrives at their house disguised as his valet and falls in love with Angelina. Dandini, his valet, arrives disguised as the prince, and the stepsisters try to charm him. He invites them all to a ball. Alidoro, the prince's tutor, uses his magical powers so that Angelina can go to the ball, too.

At the ball, Prince Ramiro sees a veiled lady who reminds him of Angelina. She gives him a bracelet and keeps one just like it for herself, saying that if he loves her, he'll find her. Later, Prince Ramiro goes to Don Magnifico's house as the prince he really is, and he recognizes the bracelet Angelina is wearing. Angelina marries the prince and asks him to forgive her stepfather and stepsisters for their mean behavior.

Il barbiere di Siviglia
(The Barber of Seville, 1816)

17th-century Seville, Spain. Count Almaviva is in love with Rosina, who lives with her guardian, Dr. Bartolo. Figaro, the town barber, offers to help Almaviva win Rosina—but it won't be easy, because Bartolo wants to marry her himself. Almaviva serenades Rosina and tells her his name is Lindoro. Rosina returns his love and sends him a note.

Almaviva arrives at Bartolo's house disguised as a music master and gives Rosina a singing lesson. Figaro comes to give Bartolo a haircut while Almaviva and Rosina plan to elope. The real music master, Don Basilio, arrives and tells Bartolo that the imposter is really Almaviva. Bartolo shows Rosina the note she wrote to "Lindoro," who, Bartolo says, left it at a girlfriend's house. Furious, Rosina agrees to marry Bartolo. But then Almaviva tells her who he

really is, Rosina is thrilled, and the lovers marry. When Bartolo discovers that Rosina has no dowry, he gives his blessing to the marriage.

Johann Strauss (1825–99)
German

Die Fledermaus
(The Bat, 1874)

19th-century Vienna, Austria. Alfred sings a serenade to Rosalinde, the wife of Eisenstein. Eisenstein has to go to jail soon for getting into a fight with a policeman. His friend Dr. Falke comes to take him to a party. When they leave, Rosalinde and Alfred have supper. Frank, the jail warden, comes to take Eisenstein to jail, and Rosalinde pretends Alfred is her husband, so Frank takes Alfred to jail instead.

At the party, Falke tells the guests how he and Eisenstein went once to a costume ball, where Falke was dressed as a bat. Afterward, Eisenstein left him drunk in a park, and when he woke up the next morning, people were making fun of his bat costume. Now, to get even, Falke has invited Rosalinde's maid Adele, Frank, and Rosalinde herself to the party—they're all disguised as other people, and they play tricks on Eisenstein, who's also disguised. Finally, everyone goes to the jail, where they reveal their identities and forgive each other.

Richard Strauss (1864–1949)
German

Der Rosenkavalier
(The Cavalier of the Rose, 1911)

18th-century Vienna, Austria. Octavian is the lover of the Marschallin (the field marshal's wife), who's about ten years older than he is. They are in the Marschallin's house when her tiresome cousin, Baron Ochs, arrives. Octavian quickly puts on a maid's outfit and pretends to be "Mariandel." Ochs flirts with "Mariandel" and tells the Marschallin he's engaged to a young girl named Sophie von Faninal, whom he's never met. According to custom, someone has to deliver a silver rose to her. The Marschallin suggests Octavian.

Octavian takes the silver rose to Sophie, and they immediately fall in love. When Sophie meets Baron Ochs, she can't stand him. Octavian tells Ochs that Sophie won't marry him, but Sophie's father, Faninal, insists. So Octavian arranges with two servants to trick Ochs. He meets Ochs at an inn, dressed up again as "Mariandel." Spooky faces pop out of doors to scare Ochs, and a woman comes in with a dozen children, saying that Ochs abandoned them. Sophie and her father arrive and see how foolish Ochs looks. The Marschallin arrives and understands that she has lost Octavian. She leaves with dignity as the two young people embrace.

Giuseppe Verdi (1813–1901)
Italian

Aida (1871)

Egypt, in the time of the pharaohs. The Egyptians and Ethiopians are at war, and the Ethiopian princess Aida has been captured and is a slave to Amneris, daughter of the king of Egypt. The leader of the Egyptian military is Radames, and he and Aida love each other. But Amneris also loves Radames,

and when she discovers Aida loves him, she gets angry and jealous.

The king of Egypt decides that Radames will marry Amneris. The unhappy Aida asks Radames to meet her, then asks him to flee with her and her father, Amonasro, to Ethiopia. Radames refuses at first, then agrees, but they are stopped and Radames is arrested. Amneris tells Radames she will save him if he will marry her, but he says he loves only Aida. Radames is condemned to die in a tomb. There, Aida joins him, and they die together.

La Traviata
(The Lost One, 1853)

19th-century Paris and the French countryside. Violetta, a courtesan who has tuberculosis, meets Alfredo Germont at a party, and they fall in love. Violetta gives up her life of parties and goes to live with Alfredo in the country.

A few months later, when Alfredo is out of the house, his father, the older Germont, comes to visit Violetta. He's surprised to find that she's an elegant lady and truly loves Alfredo. But the relationship between Alfredo and Violetta has created a scandal, and it's impossible for Alfredo's sister to find a respectable husband. Germont asks Violetta to leave Alfredo. Violetta reluctantly agrees, and leaves for Paris. Alfredo, not knowing why she has left, follows her there and speaks angrily to her at a party.

Later, Violetta becomes ill, and Alfredo comes to see her—his father has told him about the sacrifice she made for their family. Violetta urges Alfredo to marry and be happy, then she dies.

Rigoletto (1851)

16th-century Italy. The hunchback Rigoletto is the jester at the court of the Duke of Mantua. At a court ball, Rigoletto makes fun of a count, and the count places a curse on him. Rigoletto goes home, where his only happiness in life, his daughter Gilda, is waiting. The duke and his friends, the courtiers, think Gilda is Rigoletto's mistress, and the duke wants Gilda for himself. When Rigoletto leaves the house, the duke, in disguise, sneaks in and tells Gilda he's a poor student and says he loves her.

The courtiers kidnap Gilda and take her to the duke's palace. Rigoletto manages to find her, but by now she loves the duke. Rigoletto takes her to an inn owned by an assassin named Sparafucile. There, through a hole in the wall, they watch the duke flirt with Sparafucile's sister Maddalena. Gilda is distressed, and Rigoletto tells her to dress in men's clothes and ride to Verona, where he'll meet her. He then makes a deal with Sparafucile to kill the duke.

But Maddalena persuades her brother to spare him and kill instead the first person who comes to the inn. Gilda overhears them and decides to sacrifice herself to save the duke. She knocks at the door (in her men's clothes) and is killed. Rigoletto discovers to his horror that the curse has come true.

Richard Wagner (1813–83)
German

Die Meistersinger von Nürnberg
(The Mastersingers of Nuremberg, 1867)

16th-century Germany. Hans Sachs is the town's kind and respected cobbler. Walther, a young knight, learns that the town's group of singers, called the Mastersingers, are having a contest to see who can sing the best song, and the prize is Eva, a girl he loves. Walther decides to enter the contest, but when he auditions to take part, Beckmesser, the town clerk, disqualifies him for making too many mistakes. Plus, Beckmesser is in love with Eva himself. That night, Beckmesser comes to Eva's house to serenade her, and Sachs, who's sitting outside working on his shoes, hammers in a nail every time Beckmesser makes a mistake.

The next day, Sachs helps Walther work on his song. Beckmesser comes into the shop and finds the words to Walther's song; Sachs says he can take them. Then Eva arrives and inspires Walther to make his song even better. At the contest, Beckmesser sings first but doesn't understand how Walther's words are supposed to go, and no one understands what he's singing about. Then Walther sings his song, everyone is moved, Walther wins the contest and Eva, and he's named a Mastersinger.

Further Reading

Anderson, James. *The Harper Dictionary of Opera and Operetta.* New York: HarperCollins, 1990.

Boyden, Matthew, et al. *Opera: The Rough Guide.* New York: Rough Guides, 1997.

Camner, James. *How to Enjoy Opera.* Garden City, N.Y.: Doubleday, 1981.

Cargher, John. *How to Enjoy Opera without Really Trying.* Layton, Utah: Gibbs M. Smith/ Peregrine Smith Books, 1987.

Forman, Denis. *A Night at the Opera: An Irreverent Guide to the Plots, the Singers, the Composers, the Recordings.* Rev. ed. New York: Modern Library, 1998.

Goulding, Phil G. *Ticket to the Opera: Discovering and Exploring 100 Famous Works, History, Lore, and Singers, with Recommended Recordings.* New York: Fawcett, 1999.

Grout, Donald Jay. *A Short History of Opera.* 2nd ed. New York: Columbia University Press, 1965.

Gruber, Paul, ed. *The Metropolitan Opera Guide to Opera on Video.* New York: Norton, 1997.

Harewood, George Henry Hubert Lascelles, Earl of. *Kobbé's Illustrated Opera Book: Twenty Six of the World's Favorite Operas.* New York: Putnam, 1989.

Jefferson, Alan. *The Glory of Opera.* New York: G. P. Putnam's Sons, 1976.

Parker, Roger, ed. *The Oxford Illustrated History of Opera.* New York: Oxford University Press, 1994.

Plotkin, Fred. *Opera 101: A Complete Guide to Learning and Loving Opera.* New York: Hyperion, 1994.

Sacher, Jack. *Opera: A Listener's Guide.* New York: Schirmer Books, 1997.

Somerset-Ward, Richard. *The Story of Opera.* New York: Abrams, 1998.

Vickers, Hugh. *Great Operatic Disasters.* New York: St. Martin's Press, 1979.

Warrack, John Hamilton, and Ewan West. *The Concise Oxford Dictionary of Opera.* 3rd ed. New York: Oxford University Press, 1996.

OPERA SYNOPSES

Freeman, John W. *The Metropolitan Opera Stories of the Great Operas.* New York: Norton, 1996.

Geras, Adele. *The Random House Book of Opera Stories* New York: Random House, 1998.

Husain, Shahrukh. *The Barefoot Book of Stories from the Opera.* New York: Barefoot Books, 1999.

Rosenberg, Jane. *Sing Me a Story: The Metropolitan Opera's Book of Opera Stories for Children.* New York: Thames and Hudson, 1996.

Index